Kim —
Many Blessings
May God Hold —
You always in the
palm of his hand

God Bless
Fr Cory

WORDS OF ETERNAL LIFE

A Thought a Day from the Book of Sirach

WORDS OF ETERNAL LIFE

A Thought a Day from the Book of Sirach

Compiled by the
Daughters of St. Paul

ST. PAUL EDITIONS

The quotations from the book of Sirach contained in this volume were taken from the following sources:

From January 1 to March 31 and July 1 to September 30:
    The Bible text in this publication is from the Revised Standard Version Bible, Catholic Edition, copyrighted © 1965 and 1966 by the Division of Christian Education of the National Council of the Churches of Christ in the U.S.A., and used by permission.

Imprimatur: ✠ Peter W. Bartholome, D.D., Bishop of Saint Cloud, Minnesota

From April 1 to June 30:
    Scripture texts used in this work are taken from the *New American Bible,* copyright © 1970, by the Confraternity of Christian Doctrine, Washington, D.C., and are used by permission of copyright owner. All rights reserved.

Imprimatur: ✠ Patrick Cardinal O'Boyle, D.D., Archbishop of Washington

From October 1 to December 31:
    Excerpts from *The Jerusalem Bible,* copyright © 1966 by Darton, Longman & Todd, Ltd. and Doubleday and Company, Inc. Used by permission of the publisher.

Imprimatur: ✠ John Cardinal Heenan, Westminster

Herb Basso: 99
Rev. G. Colton: 43, 49, 51, 83, 103, 113, 121, 127
DSP: 11, 13, 17, 19, 21, 23, 25, 27, 31, 33, 35, 39, 41, 45, 55, 57, 61, 63, 65, 67, 69, 71, 73, 75, 79, 81, 85, 87, 89, 91, 93, 97, 101, 107, 109, 111, 117, 119, 129, 133, 135, 137, 139
Suzette Scherer: 29, 53, 77, 87, 115
V. Mancusi: 105
Pilgrim Productions: 37, 47, 125
Dennis W. Rizzo: 131
Verga: 59, 95

ISBN 0-8198-8210-0 c

Printed in the U.S.A. by the Daughters of St. Paul
50 St. Paul's Ave., Boston, MA 02130

The Daughters of St. Paul are an international congregation of women religious serving the Church with the communications media.

Introduction

The author of the book of Sirach, from which these selections have been taken, was Ben Sira, a sage who lived in Jerusalem. He wrote the book in Hebrew, probably between the years 200 and 175 B.C. The author's grandson translated it into Greek some time after 132 B.C.

Ben Sira had studied the Scriptures with love and diligence, and he was so enriched by them that he felt the need to communicate what he had learned to his countrymen. His love for the Law, the Temple, divine worship and the priesthood led him to write a synthesis of revealed religion and natural wisdom.

The book is divided into sections. The first could be considered an anthology of concise thoughts—moral lessons for all (chapters 1—43). The second contains praises of the heroes of Israel (44:1—50:21), and expresses the hope that they may have successors in the difficult times in which the author writes—the eve of the Maccabean revolt. A canticle of gratitude to the goodness of God closes this book (50:22—51:30), with an appeal to all to acquire true wisdom.

The book of Sirach gives rules for a peaceful and happy life based on an unlimited trust in God, the God who continuously intervenes with fatherly love in favor of His faithful people.

The fear of the Lord is glory and exultation,
   and gladness and a crown of rejoicing. (1:11)

The fear of the Lord delights the heart,
   and gives gladness and joy and long life. (1:12)

With him who fears the Lord it will go well at the end;
   on the day of his death he will be blessed. (1:13)

To fear the Lord is the beginning of wisdom. (1:14)

To fear the Lord is wisdom's full measure;
   she satisfies men with her fruits;
she fills their whole house with desirable goods,
   and their storehouses with her produce. (1:16-17)

To fear the Lord is the root of wisdom,
   and her branches are long life. (1:20)

Unrighteous anger cannot be justified,
   for a man's anger tips the scale to his ruin. (1:22)

A patient man will endure until the right moment,
   and then joy will burst forth for him. (1:23)

If you desire wisdom, keep the commandments,
   and the Lord will supply it for you.
For the fear of the Lord is wisdom and instruction,
   and he delights in fidelity and meekness. (1:26-27)

Do not disobey the fear of the Lord;
   do not approach him with a divided mind. (1:28)

Be not a hypocrite in men's sight,
   and keep watch over your lips. (1:29)

Do not exalt yourself lest you fall,
   and thus bring dishonor upon yourself. (1:30)

My son, if you come forward to serve the Lord,
prepare yourself for temptation. (2:1)

Set your heart right and be steadfast,
   and do not be hasty in time of calamity.
Cleave to him and do not depart,
   that you may be honored at the end of your life.
                                        (2:2-3)

Accept whatever is brought upon you,
  and in changes that humble you be patient.
For gold is tested in the fire,
  and acceptable men in the furnace of humiliation.

(2:4-5)

Trust in him, and he will help you;
  make your ways straight, and hope in him. (2:6)

You who fear the Lord, wait for his mercy;
  and turn not aside, lest you fall.
You who fear the Lord, trust in him,
  and your reward will not fail;
you who fear the Lord, hope for good things,
  for everlasting joy and mercy. (2:7-9)

Consider the ancient generations and see:
  who ever trusted in the Lord and was put to
    shame?
Or who ever persevered in the fear of the Lord and
    was forsaken?
  Or who ever called upon him and was overlooked?

(2:10)

The Lord is compassionate and merciful;
  he forgives sins and saves in time of affliction.

(2:11)

Woe to timid hearts and to slack hands,
  and to the sinner who walks along two ways!
Woe to the faint heart, for it has no trust!
  Therefore it will not be sheltered. (2:12-13)

Woe to you who have lost your endurance!
  What will you do when the Lord punishes you?
                                                    (2:14)

Those who fear the Lord will not disobey his words,
  and those who love him will keep his ways. (2:15)

Those who fear the Lord will seek his approval,
  and those who love him will be filled with the law.
                                                    (2:16)

Those who fear the Lord will prepare their hearts,
  and will humble themselves before him. (2:17)

Let us fall into the hands of the Lord,
  but not into the hands of men;
for as his majesty is,
  so also is his mercy. (2:18)

Listen to your father, O children;
  and act accordingly, that you may be kept in
    safety.
For the Lord honored the father above the children,
  and he confirmed the right of the mother over her
    sons. (3:1-2)

Whoever honors his father atones for sins,
  and whoever glorifies his mother is like one who
    lays up treasure. (3:3-4)

Whoever honors his father will be gladdened by his
    own children,
  and when he prays he will be heard. (3:5)

Whoever glorifies his father will have long life,
  and whoever obeys the Lord will refresh his
    mother;
  he will serve his parents as his masters. (3:6-7)

Honor your father by word and deed,
  that a blessing from him may come upon you.
For a father's blessing strengthens the houses of the
    children,
  but a mother's curse uproots their foundations.

(3:8-9)

O son, help your father in his old age,
and do not grieve him as long as he lives;
even if he is lacking in understanding, show
forbearance;
in all your strength do not despise him. (3:12-13)

My son, perform your tasks in meekness;
then you will be loved by those whom God
accepts. (3:17)

The greater you are, the more you must humble
yourself;
so you will find favor in the sight of the Lord.
For great is the might of the Lord;
he is glorified by the humble. (3:18-20)

Seek not what is too difficult for you,
nor investigate what is beyond your power.
Reflect upon what has been assigned to you,
for you do not need what is hidden. (3:21-22)

Do not meddle in what is beyond your tasks,
  for matters too great for human understanding
    have been shown you.
For their hasty judgment has led many astray,
  and wrong opinion has caused their thoughts to
    slip. (3:23-24)

A stubborn mind will be afflicted at the end,
  and whoever loves danger will perish by it. (3:26)

Water extinguishes a blazing fire:
  so almsgiving atones for sin. (3:30)

Whoever requites favors gives thought to the future;
  at the moment of his falling he will find support.
                                                    (3:31)

My son, deprive not the poor of his living,
  and do not keep needy eyes waiting.
Do not grieve the one who is hungry,
  nor anger a man in want. (4:1-2)

Do not add to the troubles of an angry mind,
  nor delay your gift to a beggar.
Do not reject an afflicted suppliant,
  nor turn your face away from the poor. (4:3-4)

Incline your ear to the poor,
  and answer him peaceably and gently. (4:8)

Deliver him who is wronged from the hand of the
    wrongdoer;
  and do not be fainthearted in judging a case. (4:9)

Be like a father to orphans,
  and instead of a husband to their mother;
you will then be like a son of the Most High,
  and he will love you more than does your mother.

(4:10)

Wisdom exalts her sons
  and gives help to those who seek her.
Whoever loves her loves life,
  and those who seek her early will be filled with joy.

(4:11)

Do not show partiality, to your own harm,
  or deference, to your downfall. (4:22)

Do not refrain from speaking at the crucial time,
  and do not hide your wisdom.
For wisdom is known through speech,
  and education through the words of the tongue.
(4:23-24)

Never speak against the truth,
  but be mindful of your ignorance. (4:25)

Do not be ashamed to confess your sins. (4:26)

Strive even to death for the truth
and the Lord God will fight for you. (4:28)

Do not be reckless in your speech,
  or sluggish and remiss in your deeds. (4:29)

Do not say, "I sinned, and what happened to me?"
  for the Lord is slow to anger.
Do not be so confident of atonement
  that you add sin to sin. (5:4-5)

February 21

Do not delay to turn to the Lord,
    nor postpone it from day to day;
for suddenly the wrath of the Lord will go forth,
    and at the time of punishment you will perish. (5:7)

February 22

Be steadfast in your understanding,
    and let your speech be consistent.
Be quick to hear,
    and be deliberate in answering. (5:10-11)

February 23

When you gain a friend, gain him through testing,
    and do not trust him hastily.
For there is a friend who is such at his own
        convenience,
    but will not stand by you in your day of trouble.
(6:7-8)

February 24

A faithful friend is a sturdy shelter:
    he that has found one has found a treasure. (6:14)

February 25

There is nothing so precious as a faithful friend,
    and no scales can measure his excellence. (6:15)

February 26

My son, from your youth up choose instruction,
    and until you are old you will keep finding wisdom.
(6:18)

If you are willing, my son, you will be taught,
and if you apply yourself you will become clever.
If you love to listen you will gain knowledge,
and if you incline your ear you will become wise.

(6:32-33)

Reflect on the statutes of the Lord,
and meditate at all times on his commandments.
It is he who will give insight to your mind,
and your desire for wisdom will be granted. (6:37)

Do no evil, and evil will never befall you.
Stay away from wrong, and it will turn away from
you. (7:1-2)

Do not commit a sin twice;
even for one you will not go unpunished.
Do not say, "He will consider the multitude of my
gifts,
and when I make an offering to the Most High God
he will accept it." (7:8-9)

Do not be fainthearted in your prayer,
nor neglect to give alms. (7:10)

March 4

Do not ridicule a man who is bitter in soul,
  for there is One who abases and exalts. (7:11)

March 5

Do you have children? Discipline them,
  and make them obedient from their youth. (7:23)

March 6

Do you have daughters? Be concerned for their
    chastity,
  and do not show yourself too indulgent with them.
                                                  (7:24)

March 7

With all your heart honor your father,
  and do not forget the birth pangs of your mother.
Remember that through your parents you were born;
  and what can you give back to them that equals
    their gift to you? (7:27-28)

March 8

Stretch forth your hand to the poor,
  so that your blessing may be complete. (7:32)

March 9

Give graciously to all the living,
  and withhold not kindness from the dead.
Do not fail those who weep,
  but mourn with those who mourn. (7:33-34)

March 10

Do not shrink from visiting a sick man,
    because for such deeds you will be loved. (7:35)

March 11

In all you do, remember the end of your life,
    and then you will never sin. (7:36)

March 12

Do not disregard the discourse of the aged,
    for they themselves learned from their fathers;
because from them you will gain understanding
    and learn how to give an answer in time of need.
(8:9)

March 13

Forsake not an old friend,
    for a new one does not compare with him.
A new friend is like new wine;
    when it has aged you will drink it with pleasure.
(9:10)

March 14

Do not envy the honors of a sinner,
    for you do not know what his end will be. (9:11)

March 15

As much as you can, aim to know your neighbors,
    and consult with the wise. (9:14)

Let your conversation be with men of understanding,
and let all your discussion be about the law of the
Most High. (9:15)

Do not be angry with your neighbor for any injury,
and do not attempt anything by acts of insolence.
Arrogance is hateful before the Lord and before
men,
and injustice is outrageous to both. (10:6-7)

The beginning of man's pride is to depart from the
Lord;
his heart has forsaken his Maker.
For the beginning of pride is sin,
and the man who clings to it pours out
abominations. (10:12-13)

Pride was not created for men,
nor fierce anger for those born of women. (10:18)

What race is worthy of honor? The human race.
What race is worthy of honor? Those who fear the
Lord.
What race is unworthy of honor? The human race.
What race is unworthy of honor? Those who
transgress the commandments. (10:19)

The rich, and the eminent, and the poor—
   their glory is the fear of the Lord. (10:22)

The nobleman, and the judge, and the ruler will be
   honored,
   but none of them is greater than the man who
   fears the Lord. (10:24)

Do not make a display of your wisdom when you do
   your work,
   nor glorify yourself at a time when you are in want.
Better is a man who works and has an abundance of
   everything,
   than one who goes about boasting, but lacks
   bread. (10:26-27)

My son, glorify yourself with humility,
   and ascribe to yourself honor according to your
   worth. (10:28)

The wisdom of a humble man will lift up his head,
   and will seat him among the great. (11:1)

Do not find fault before you investigate;
   first consider, and then reprove. (11:7)

March 27

Do not wonder at the works of a sinner,
  but trust in the Lord and keep at your toil....
For it is easy in the sight of the Lord
  to reward a man on the day of death according to
    his conduct. (11:21, 26)

March 28

Do good to a godly man, and you will be repaid—
  if not by him, certainly by the Most High. (12:2)

March 29

Blessed is he whose heart does not condemn him,
  and who has not given up his hope. (14:2)

March 30

Do good to a friend before you die,
  and reach out and give to him as much as you
    can....
Will you not leave the fruit of your labors to another,
  and what you acquired by toil to be divided by lot?
    (14:13, 15)

March 31

All living beings become old like a garment,
  for the decree from of old is, "You must surely
    die!"
Like flourishing leaves on a spreading tree
  which sheds some and puts forth others,
so are the generations of flesh and blood:
  one dies and another is born. (14:17-18)

Happy the man who meditates on wisdom,
   and reflects on knowledge;
Who ponders her ways in his heart,
   and understands her paths. (14:20-21)

Say not: "It was God's doing that I fell away";
   for what he hates he does not do.
Say not: "It was he who set me astray";
   for he has no need of wicked man. (15:11-12)

Abominable wickedness the Lord hates,
   he does not let it befall those who fear him. (15:13)

When God, in the beginning, created man,
   he made him subject to his own free choice. (15:14)

If you choose you can keep the commandments;
   it is loyalty to do his will. (15:15)

There are set before you fire and water;
   to whichever you choose, stretch forth your hand.
(15:16)

Before man are life and death,
   whichever he chooses shall be given him. (15:17)

Immense is the wisdom of the Lord;
   he is mighty in power, and all-seeing.
The eyes of God see all he has made;
   he understands man's every deed.
No man does he command to sin,
   to none does he give strength for lies. (15:18-20)

Whoever does good has his reward,
   which each receives according to his deeds. (16:14)

Say not: "I am hidden from God;
   in heaven who remembers me?
Among so many people I cannot be known;
   what am I in the world of spirits?"
Such are the thoughts of senseless men,
   which only the foolish knave will think. (16:15, 21)

When at the first God created his works
   and, as he made them, assigned their tasks,
He ordered for all time what they were to do
   and their domains from generation to generation.
They were not to hunger, nor grow weary,
   nor ever cease from their tasks. (16:24-25)

The Lord from the earth created man,
   and in his own image he made him.
Limited days of life he gives him
   and makes him return to earth again. (17:1-2)

He endows man with a strength of his own,
   and with power over all things else on earth.
He puts the fear of him in all flesh,
   and gives him rule over beasts and birds. (17:3-4)

He forms men's tongues and eyes and ears,
   and imparts to them an understanding heart. (17:5)

With wisdom and knowledge he fills them;
   good and evil he shows them. (17:6)

He looks with favor upon their hearts,
   and shows them his glorious works,
That they may describe the wonders of his deeds
   and praise his holy name. (17:7-8)

He has set before them knowledge,
   a law of life as their inheritance;
An everlasting covenant he has made with them,
   his commandments he has revealed to them.

(17:9-10)

His majestic glory their eyes beheld,
  his glorious voice their ears heard.
He says to them, "Avoid all evil";
  each of them he gives precepts about his fellow
    men. (17:11-12)

Their ways are ever known to him,
  they cannot be hidden from his eyes. (17:13)

All their actions are clear as the sun to him,
  his eyes are ever upon their ways. (17:15)

Later he will rise up and repay them,
  and requite each one of them as they deserve.
                                              (17:18)

But to the penitent he provides a way back,
  he encourages those who are losing hope! (17:19)

How great the mercy of the Lord,
  his forgiveness of those who return to him! (17:24)

The Eternal is the judge of all things without
    exception;
  the Lord alone is just. (18:1)

Whom has he made equal to describing his works,
and who can probe his mighty deeds? (18:2)

Who can measure his majestic power,
or exhaust the tale of his mercies? (18:3)

One cannot lessen, nor increase,
nor penetrate the wonders of the Lord. (18:4)

The sum of a man's days is great
if it reaches a hundred years:
Like a drop of sea water, like a grain of sand,
so are these few years among the days of eternity.

(18:7-8)

That is why the Lord is patient with men
and showers upon them his mercy.
He sees and understands that their death is
grievous,
and so he forgives them all the more. (18:9-10)

Man may be merciful to his fellow man,
　　but the Lord's mercy reaches all flesh,
Reproving, admonishing, teaching,
　　as a shepherd guides his flock;
Merciful to those who accept his guidance,
　　who are diligent in his precepts. (18:11-13)

May 1

My son, to your charity add no reproach,
　　nor spoil any gift by harsh words.
Like dew that abates a burning wind,
　　so does a word improve a gift. (18:14-15)

May 2

Be informed before speaking;
　　before sickness prepare the cure. (18:18)

May 3

Before you have fallen, humble yourself;
　　when you have sinned, show repentance. (18:20)

May 4

Let nothing prevent the prompt payment of your
　　vows;
　　wait not to fulfill them when you are dying. (18:22)

May 5

Before making a vow have the means to fulfill it;
　　be not one who tries the Lord. (18:23)

Remember the time of hunger in the time of plenty,
poverty and want in the day of wealth. (18:25)

A wise man is circumspect in all things;
when sin is rife he keeps himself from wrongdoing.
(18:27)

Any learned man should make wisdom known,
and he who attains to her should declare her
praise;
Those trained in her words must show their wisdom,
dispensing sound proverbs like lifegiving waters.
(18:28-29)

Go not after your lusts,
but keep your desires in check. (18:30)

He who gloats over evil will meet with evil,
and he who repeats an evil report has no sense.
(19:5)

Never repeat gossip,
and you will not be reviled. (19:6)

Let anything you hear die within you;
  be assured it will not make you burst. (19:9)

Like an arrow lodged in a man's thigh
  is gossip in the breast of a fool. (19:11)

Admonish your friend—he may not have done it;
  and if he did, that he may not do it again. (19:12)

Admonish your neighbor—he may not have said it;
  and if he did, that he may not say it again....
Then, too, a man can slip and not mean it;
  who has not sinned with his tongue? (19:13, 15)

Admonish your neighbor before you break with him;
  thus will you fulfill the law of the Most High. (19:16)

All wisdom is fear of the Lord;
  perfect wisdom is the fulfillment of the law. (19:17)

The knowledge of wickedness is not wisdom,
  nor is there prudence in the counsel of sinners.
There is a shrewdness that is detestable,
  while the simple man may be free from sin.

                      (19:18-19)

There are those with little understanding who fear
  God,
  and those of great intelligence who violate the law.
(19:20)

An admonition can be inopportune,
  and a man may be wise to hold his peace. (20:1)

It is much better to admonish than to lose one's
  temper,
  for one who admits his fault will be kept from
  disgrace. (20:2)

A wise man is silent till the right time comes,
  but a boasting fool ignores the proper time. (20:6)

He who talks too much is detested;
  he who pretends to authority is hated. (20:7)

Some misfortunes bring success;
  some things gained are a man's loss. (20:8)

Humiliation can follow fame,
  while from obscurity a man can lift up his head.
(20:10)

A wise man makes himself popular by a few words,
  but fools pour forth their blandishments in vain.

(20:12)

My son, if you have sinned, do so no mcre,
  and for your past sins pray to be forgiven. (21:1)

Flee from sin as from a serpent
  that will bite you if you go near it;
Its teeth are lion's teeth,
  destroying the souls of men. (21:2)

Every offense is a two-edged sword;
  when it cuts, there can be no healing. (21:3)

He who hates correction walks the sinner's path,
  but he who fears the Lord repents in his heart.

(21:6)

Widely known is the boastful speaker,
  but the wise man knows his own faults. (21:7)

He who builds his house with another's money
  is collecting stones for his funeral mound. (21:8)

The path of sinners is smooth stones
that end in the depths of the nether world. (21:10)

He who keeps the law controls his impulses;
he who is perfect in fear of the Lord has wisdom.

(21:11)

A wise man's knowledge wells up in a flood,
and his counsel, like a living spring;
A fool's mind is like a broken jar—
no knowledge at all can it hold. (21:13-14)

When an intelligent man hears words of wisdom,
he approves them and adds to them;
The wanton hears them with scorn
and casts them behind his back. (21:15)

The views of a prudent man are sought in an
assembly,
and his words are considered with care. (21:16)

Like fetters on the legs is learning to a fool,
like a manacle on his right hand. (21:19)

A fool raises his voice in laughter,
but a prudent man at the most smiles gently. (21:20)

The lips of the impious talk of what is not their
concern,
but the words of the prudent are carefully weighed.
(21:25)

Fools' thoughts are in their mouths,
wise men's words are in their hearts. (21:26)

A slanderer besmirches himself,
and is hated by his neighbors. (21:28)

Masonry bonded with wooden beams
is not loosened by an earthquake;
Neither is a resolve constructed with careful
deliberation
shaken in a moment of fear. (22:16)

A resolve that is backed by prudent understanding
is like the polished surface of a smooth wall. (22:17)

Small stones lying on an open height
  will not remain when the wind blows;
Neither can a timid resolve based on foolish plans
  withstand fear of any kind. (22:18)

He who throws stones at birds drives them away
  and he who insults a friend breaks up the
    friendship. (22:20)

From a friend in need of support
  no one need hide in shame;
But from him who brings harm to his friend
  all will stand aloof who hear of it. (22:25-26)

Who will set a guard over my mouth,
  and upon my lips an effective seal,
That I may not fail through them,
  that my tongue may not destroy me? (22:27)

Who will apply the lash to my thoughts,
    to my mind the rod of discipline,
That my failings may not be spared,
    nor the sins of my heart overlooked;
Lest my failings increase,
    and my sins be multiplied;
Lest I succumb to my foes,
    and my enemy rejoice over me?
Lord, Father and God of my life,
    abandon me not into their control! (23:2-4)

A brazen look allow me not;
    ward off passion from my heart,
Let not the lustful cravings of the flesh master me,
    surrender me not to shameless desires. (23:5-6)

Give heed, my children, to the instruction that I
    pronounce,
    for he who keeps it will not be enslaved.
Through his lips is the sinner ensnared;
    the railer and the arrogant man fall thereby. (23:7-8)

Let not your mouth form the habit of swearing,
    or becoming too familiar with the Holy Name. (23:9)

Let not your mouth become used to coarse talk,
  for in it lies sinful matter. (23:13)

A man who has the habit of abusive language
  will never mature in character as long as he lives.
  (23:15)

Wisdom sings her own praises,
  before her own people she proclaims her glory;
In the assembly of the Most High she opens her
    mouth,
  in the presence of his hosts she declares her
    worth:
"From the mouth of the Most High I came forth,
  and mistlike covered the earth.
In the highest heavens did I dwell,
  my throne on a pillar of cloud." (24:1-4)

"The vault of heaven I compassed alone,
  through the deep abyss I wandered.
Over waves of the sea, over all the land,
  over every people and nation I held sway.
Among all these I sought a resting place;
  in whose inheritance should I abide?" (24:5-7)

"Then the Creator of all gave me his command,
 and he who formed me chose the spot for my tent,
Saying, 'In Jacob make your dwelling,
 in Israel your inheritance.'" (24:8)

"Before all ages, in the beginning, he created me,
 and through all ages I shall not cease to be.
In the holy tent I ministered before him,
 and in Zion I fixed my abode." (24:9-10)

"Come to me, all you that yearn for me,
 and be filled with my fruits;
You will remember me as sweeter than honey,
 better to have than the honeycomb." (24:18-19)

"He who eats of me will hunger still,
 he who drinks of me will thirst for more;
He who obeys me will not be put to shame,
 he who serves me will never fail." (24:20-21)

The first man never finished comprehending
 wisdom,
 nor will the last succeed in fathoming her.
For deeper than the sea are her thoughts;
 her counsels, than the great abyss. (24:26-27)

My soul takes pleasure in three things,
  and they are beautiful in the sight of the Lord and
    of men:
agreement between brothers, friendship between
  neighbors,
  and a wife and husband who live in harmony. (25:1)

How attractive is wisdom in the aged,
  and understanding and counsel in honorable men!
                                                    (25:5)

Rich experience is the crown of the aged,
  and their boast is the fear of the Lord. (25:6)

How great is he who has gained wisdom!
  But there is no one superior to him who fears the
    Lord. (25:10)

The fear of the Lord surpasses everything;
  to whom shall be likened the one who holds it fast?
                                                    (25:11)

Happy is the husband of a good wife;
  the number of his days will be doubled.
A loyal wife rejoices her husband,
  and he will complete his years in peace. (26:1-2)

Keep strict watch over a headstrong daughter,
lest, when she finds liberty, she use it to her hurt.
(26:10)

A silent wife is a gift of the Lord,
and there is nothing so precious as a disciplined
soul. (26:14)

A modest wife adds charm to charm,
and no balance can weigh the value of a chaste
soul. (26:15)

Like the sun rising in the heights of the Lord,
so is the beauty of a good wife in her well-ordered
home. (26:16)

At two things my heart is grieved,
and because of a third anger comes over me:
a warrior in want through poverty,
and intelligent men who are treated
contemptuously;
a man who turns back from righteousness to sin—
the Lord will prepare him for the sword! (26:28)

The kiln tests the potter's vessels;
   so the test of a man is in his reasoning. (27:5)

The fruit discloses the cultivation of a tree;
   so the expression of a thought discloses the
   cultivation of a man's mind. (27:6)

Do not praise a man before you hear him reason,
   for this is the test of men. (27:7)

If you pursue justice, you will attain it
   and wear it as a glorious robe. (27:8)

Birds flock with their kind;
   so truth returns to those who practice it. (27:9)

A lion lies in wait for prey;
   so does sin for the workers of iniquity. (27:10)

The talk of the godly man is always wise,
   but the fool changes like the moon. (27:11)

Whoever betrays secrets destroys confidence,
   and he will never find a congenial friend. (27:16)

Love your friend and keep faith with him;
    but if you betray his secrets, do not run after him....
For a wound may be bandaged,
    and there is reconciliation after abuse,
but whoever has betrayed secrets is without hope.

(27:17, 21)

He who digs a pit will fall into it,
    and he who sets a snare will be caught in it. (27:26)

If a man does evil, it will roll back upon him,
    and he will not know where it came from. (27:27)

Those who rejoice in the fall of the godly will be
        caught in a snare,
    and pain will consume them before their death.

(27:29)

He that takes vengeance will suffer vengeance from
        the Lord,
    and he will firmly establish his sins. (28:1)

Forgive your neighbor the wrong he has done,
    and then your sins will be pardoned when you
        pray. (28:2)

Does a man harbor anger against another,
and yet seek for healing from the Lord?
Does he have no mercy toward a man like himself,
and yet pray for his own sins? (28:3-4)

If he himself, being flesh, maintains wrath,
who will make expiation for his sins? (28:5)

Remember the end of your life, and cease from
enmity,
remember destruction and death, and be true to
the commandments. (28:6)

Remember the commandments, and do not be
angry with your neighbor;
remember the covenant of the Most High, and
overlook ignorance. (28:7)

Curse the whisperer and deceiver,
for he has destroyed many who were at peace.

(28:13)

Slander has shaken many,
  and scattered them from nation to nation,
and destroyed strong cities,
  and overturned the houses of great men. (28:14)

Whoever pays heed to slander will not find rest,
  nor will he settle down in peace.
The blow of a whip raises a welt,
  but a blow of the tongue crushes the bones.

(28:16-17)

Many have fallen by the edge of the sword,
  but not so many as have fallen because of the
    tongue. (28:18)

He that shows mercy will lend to his neighbor,
  and he that strengthens him with his hand keeps
    the commandments. (29:1)

Lend to your neighbor in the time of his need;
  and in turn, repay your neighbor promptly. (29:2)

Help a poor man for the commandment's sake,
  and because of his need do not send him away
    empty. (29:9)

Lose your silver for the sake of a brother or a friend,
and do not let it rust under a stone and be lost.

(29:10)

Lay up your treasure according to the
commandments of the Most High,
and it will profit you more than gold. (29:11)

Store up almsgiving in your treasury,
and it will rescue you from all affliction;
more than a mighty shield and more than a heavy
spear,
it will fight on your behalf against your enemy.

(29:12-13)

Better is the life of a poor man under the shelter of
his roof
than sumptuous food in another man's house.

(29:22)

He who disciplines his son will profit by him,
and will boast of him among acquaintances. (30:2)

He who teaches his son will make his enemies
envious,
and will glory in him in the presence of friends.

(30:3)

A horse that is untamed turns out to be stubborn,
and a son unrestrained turns out to be willful. (30:8)

Discipline your son and take pains with him,
that you may not be offended by his
shamelessness. (30:13)

Gladness of heart is the life of man,
and the rejoicing of a man is length of days. (30:22)

Delight your soul and comfort your heart,
and remove sorrow far from you,
for sorrow has destroyed many,
and there is no profit in it. (30:23)

Jealousy and anger shorten life,
and anxiety brings on old age too soon. (30:24)

Wakefulness over wealth wastes away one's
flesh,
and anxiety about it removes sleep. (31:1)

He who loves gold will not be justified,
and he who pursues money will be led astray by it.
(31:5)

Many have come to ruin because of gold,
and their destruction has met them face to face.

(31:6)

Blessed is the rich man who is found blameless,
and who does not go after gold.
Who is he? And we will call him blessed,
for he has done wonderful things among his
people. (31:8-9)

Who has had the power to transgress and did not
transgress,
and to do evil and did not do it?
His prosperity will be established,
and the assembly will relate his acts of charity.

(31:10-11)

Judge your neighbor's feelings by your own,
and in every matter be thoughtful. (31:15)

In all your work be industrious,
and no sickness will overtake you. (31:22)

Wine drunk in season and temperately
  is rejoicing of heart and gladness of soul.
Wine drunk to excess is bitterness of soul,
  with provocation and stumbling. (31:28-29)

Speak concisely, say much in few words;
  be as one who knows and yet holds his tongue.
(32:8)

Among the great do not act as their equal;
  and when another is speaking, do not babble. (32:9)

He who fears the Lord will accept his discipline,
  and those who rise early to seek him will find favor.
(32:14)

He who seeks the law will be filled with it,
  but the hypocrite will stumble at it. (32:15)

Those who fear the Lord will form true judgments,
  and like a light they will kindle righteous deeds.
(32:16)

A sinful man will shun reproof,
  and will find a decision according to his liking.
(32:17)

Do nothing without deliberation;
   and when you have acted, do not regret it. (32:19)

Do not be overconfident on a smooth way,
   and give good heed to your paths.
Guard yourself in every act,
   for this is the keeping of the commandments.
(32:21-23)

No evil will befall the man who fears the Lord,
   but in trial he will deliver him again and again. (33:1)

A wise man will not hate the law,
   but he who is hypocritical about it is like a boat in a
     storm. (33:2)

Prepare what to say, and thus you will be heard;
   bind together your instruction, and make your
     answer. (33:4)

All men are from the ground,
   and Adam was created of the dust.
In the fullness of his knowledge the Lord
     distinguished them
   and appointed their different ways. (33:10-11)

September 6

As clay in the hand of the potter—
   for all his ways are as he pleases—
so men are in the hand of him who made them,
   to give them as he decides. (33:13)

September 7

Good is the opposite of evil,
   and life the opposite of death;
   so the sinner is the opposite of the godly. (33:14)

September 8

Do not act immoderately toward anybody,
   and do nothing without discretion. (33:29)

September 9

From an unclean thing what will be made clean?
   And from something false what will be true? (34:4)

September 10

The spirit of those who fear the Lord will live,
   for their hope is in him who saves them. (34:13)

September 11

He who fears the Lord will not be timid,
   nor play the coward, for he is his hope. (34:14)

The eyes of the Lord are upon those who love him,
  a mighty protection and strong support,
a shelter from the hot wind and a shade from
    noonday sun,
  a guard against stumbling and a defense against
    falling. (34:16)

He lifts up the soul and gives light to the eyes;
  he grants healing, life, and blessing. (34:17)

The bread of the needy is the life of the poor;
  whoever deprives them of it is a man of blood.
                                              (34:21)

To take away a neighbor's living is to murder him;
  to deprive an employee of his wages is to shed
    blood. (34:22)

He who keeps the law makes many offerings;
  he who heeds the commandments sacrifices a
    peace offering. (35:1)

He who returns a kindness offers fine flour,
  and he who gives alms sacrifices a thank offering.
                                              (35:2)

To keep from wickedness is pleasing to the Lord,
and to forsake unrighteousness is atonement.

(35:3)

Do not appear before the Lord empty-handed,
for all these things are to be done because of the
commandment. (35:4-5)

The offering of a righteous man anoints the altar,
and its pleasing odor rises before the Most High.

(35:6)

The sacrifice of a righteous man is acceptable,
and the memory of it will not be forgotten. (35:7)

Glorify the Lord generously,
and do not stint the first fruits of your hands. (35:8)

With every gift show a cheerful face,
and dedicate your tithe with gladness. (35:9)

Give to the Most High as he has given,
and as generously as your hand has found.
For the Lord is the one who repays,
and he will repay you sevenfold. (35:10-11)

Do not offer him a bribe, for he will not accept it;
  and do not trust to an unrighteous sacrifice;
for the Lord is the judge,
  and with him is no partiality. (35:12)

He will not show partiality in the case of a poor man;
  and he will listen to the prayer of one who is
    wronged. (35:13)

He will not ignore the supplication of the fatherless,
  nor the widow when she pours out her story. (35:14)

He whose service is pleasing to the Lord will be
    accepted,
  and his prayer will reach to the clouds. (35:16)

The prayer of the humble pierces the clouds,
  and he will not be consoled until it reàches the
    Lord;
he will not desist until the Most High visits him,
  and does justice for the righteous, and executes
    judgment. (35:17)

And the Lord will not delay,
    neither will he be patient with them...
till he repays man according to his deeds,
    and the works of men according to their devices;
till he judges the case of his people
    and makes them rejoice in his mercy. (35:18-19)

October 1

Have mercy on us, Master, Lord of all, and look
        on us,
    cast the fear of yourself over every nation. (36:1)

October 2

Send new portents, do fresh wonders,
    win glory for your hand and your right arm. (36:5)

October 3

Give those who wait for you their reward,
    and let your prophets be proved worthy of belief.
                                                    (36:15)

October 4

Grant, Lord, the prayer of your servants...
so that all the earth's inhabitants may acknowledge
    that you are the Lord, the everlasting God.

                                                    (36:16-17)

The stomach takes in all kinds of food
   but some foods are better than others.
As the palate discerns the flavour of game,
   so a shrewd man detects lying words. (36:18-19)

The man who takes a wife has the makings of a
   fortune,
   a helper that suits him, and a pillar to lean on.
(36:24)

If a property has no fence, it will be plundered.
When a man has no wife, he is aimless and
   querulous. (36:25)

Will anyone trust a man carrying weapons
   who flits from town to town?
So it is with the man who has no nest,
   and lodges wherever night overtakes him. (36:26-27)

Do not forget the friend who fought your battles,
   do not put him out of mind once you are rich. (37:6)

Beware of a man who offers advice,
    first find out what he wants himself—
since his advice coincides with his own interest—
    in case he has designs on you
and tells you, "You are on the right road,"
    but stands well clear to see what will happen
        to you. (37:8-9)

Do not consult a woman about her rival,
    or a coward about war,
a merchant about prices,
    or a buyer about selling,
a mean man about gratitude,
    or a selfish man about kindness,
a lazy fellow about any sort of work,
    or a casual worker about finishing a job,
an idle servant about a major undertaking—
    do not rely on these for any advice. (37:11)

But constantly have recourse to a devout man,
    whom you know to be a keeper of the
        commandments,
whose soul matches your own,
    and who, if you go wrong, will be sympathetic.
                                        (37:12)

Finally, stick to the advice your own heart gives you,
  no one can be truer to you than that;
since a man's soul often forewarns him better
  than seven watchmen perched on a watchtower.

(37:13-14)

And besides all this beg the Most High
  to guide your steps in the truth. (37:15)

Reason must be the beginning of every activity,
  reflection must come before any undertaking.

(37:16)

Thoughts are rooted in the heart,
  and this sends out four branches:
good and evil, life and death,
  and always mistress of them all is the tongue.

(37:17-18)

Think of a clever man who teaches many people,
  but does no good at all to himself. (37:19)

Think of a man, a ready enough speaker, yet he is
    detested
  and will end up by starving,
not having won the favour of the Lord,
  and being destitute of all wisdom. (37:20-21)

The truly wise will instruct his own people,
  the fruits of his understanding are certain. (37:23)

This wise man will be filled with blessing,
  and those who see him will call him happy. (37:24)

The wise man will earn confidence among his
    people,
  his name will live for ever. (37:26)

My son, in the course of your life test your
    constitution,
  and do not allow it what you see is harmful to it;
for everything does not suit everybody,
  nor does everybody take pleasure in everything.
                                    (37:27-28)

Many have died of gluttony;
  beware of this and you will prolong your life. (37:31)

October 24

Honour the doctor with the honour that is his due
   in return for his services;
   for he too has been created by the Lord. (38:1)

October 25

Healing itself comes from the Most High,
   like a gift from a king. (38:2)

October 26

The Lord has brought medicines into existence from
      the earth,
   and the sensible man will not despise them. (38:4)

October 27

He has also given men learning
   so that they may glory in his mighty works. (38:6)

October 28

Thus there is no end to his activities,
   and through him health extends across the world.
                                                    (38:8)

October 29

My son, when you are ill, do not be depressed,
   but pray to the Lord and he will heal you. (38:9)

October 30

Renounce your faults, keep your hands unsoiled,
   and cleanse your heart from all sin. (38:10)

My son, shed tears over a dead man,
  and intone the lament to show your own deep
    grief;
bury his body with due ceremonial,
  and do not neglect to honour his grave. (38:16)

...Grief can lead to death,
  a grief-stricken heart undermines your strength.
                                        (38:18-19)

Let grief end with the funeral;
  a life of grief oppresses the mind. (38:19)

Do not abandon your heart to grief,
  drive it away, bear your own end in mind. (38:20)

"Remember my doom, since it will be yours too;
  yesterday was my day, today is yours." (38:22)

Once the dead man is laid to rest, let his memory
    rest too,
  do not fret for him, once his spirit departs. (38:23)

Listen to me, devout children, and blossom
  like the rose that grows on the bank of a
    watercourse.
Give off a sweet smell like incense,
  flower like the lily, spread your fragrance abroad,
sing a song of praise
  blessing the Lord for all his works. (39:13-14)

Declare the greatness of his name,
  proclaim his praise
with song and with lyre,
  and this is how you must sing his praises:
how wonderful they are, all the works of the Lord!
                                        (39:15)

The actions of every creature are before him,
  there is no hiding from his eyes;
his gaze stretches from eternity to eternity,
  and nothing can astonish him. (39:19-20)

You must not say, "What is this? Why is that?"
  All things have been created for their proper
    functions. (39:21)

November 10

Much hardship has been made for every man,
  a heavy yoke lies on the sons of Adam
from the day they come out of their mother's womb,
  till the day they return to the mother of them all.
                                          (40:1)

November 11

What fills them with brooding and their hearts with
    fear
  is dread of the day of death. (40:2)

November 12

For all creatures, from men to animals—
  and seven times more for sinners—
there is death and blood and strife and the sword,
  disasters, famine, affliction, plague. (40:8-9)

November 13

All bribery and injustice will be blotted out,
  but good faith will stand for ever. (40:12)

November 14

The wealth of wrong-doers will dry up like a torrent,
  will crash like a clap of thunder in a downpour.
                                          (40:13)

November 15

Graciousness is like a paradise of blessing,
  and generosity stands firm for ever. (40:17)

Children and the building of a city make a man's
    reputation;
    better than either, the discovery of wisdom. (40:19)

Wine and music cheer the heart;
    better than either, the love of wisdom. (40:20)

Gold and silver will steady your feet;
    better valued than either, good advice. (40:25)

Money and strength make a confident heart;
    better than either, the fear of the Lord.
With the fear of the Lord a man lacks nothing;
    with that he need seek no ally. (40:26)

The fear of the Lord is like a paradise of blessing,
    it clothes a man with more than glory. (40:27)

Do not dread death's sentence;
    remember those who came before you and those
    who will come after. (41:3)

November 22

This is the sentence passed on all living creatures by
the Lord,
so why object to what seems good to the Most
High? (41:4)

November 23

Be careful of your reputation, for it will last you longer
than a thousand great hoards of gold. (41:12)

November 24

A good life lasts a certain number of days,
but a good reputation lasts for ever. (41:13)

November 25

Next, I will remind you of the works of the Lord,
and tell of what I have seen.
By the words of the Lord his works come into being
and all creation obeys his will. (42:15)

November 26

As the sun in shining looks on all things,
so the work of the Lord is full of his glory. (42:16)

November 27

He declares what is past and what will be,
and uncovers the traces of hidden things. (42:19)

November 28

Not a thought escapes him,
not a single word is hidden from him. (42:20)

He has imposed an order on the magnificent works
    of his wisdom,
  he is from everlasting to everlasting,
nothing can be added to him, nothing taken away,
    he needs no one's advice. (42:21)

How desirable are all his works,
  how dazzling to the eye!
They all live and last for ever,
    whatever the circumstances all obey him. (42:22-23)

Thanks to him all ends well,
  and all things hold together by means of his word.
(43:26)

We could say much more and still fall short;
  to put it concisely, "He is all." (43:27)

Where shall we find sufficient power to glorify him,
  since he is the Great One, above all his works,
the awe-inspiring Lord, stupendously great,
  and wonderful in his power? (43:28-29)

Exalt the Lord in your praises
  as high as you may—still he surpasses you.

(43:30-a)

Exert all your strength when you exalt him,
do not grow tired—you will never come to the end.

(43:30-b)

Who has ever seen him to give a description?
Who can glorify him as he deserves? (43:31)

Many mysteries remain even greater than these,
for we have seen only a few of his works,
the Lord himself having made all things—
and having given wisdom to devout men. (43:32)

Next let us praise illustrious men,
our ancestors in their successive generations.
The Lord has created an abundance of glory,
and displayed his greatness from earliest times.

(44:1-2)

Noah was found perfectly virtuous,
in the time of wrath he became the scion:
because of him a remnant was preserved for the
earth
at the coming of the Flood. (44:17)

Abraham, the great forefather of a host of nations,
   no one was ever his equal in glory....
The Lord therefore promised him on oath
   to bless the nations through his descendants,
to multiply him like the dust on the ground,
   to exalt his descendants like the stars,
and give them the land for their inheritance,
   from sea to sea,
from the River to the ends of the earth. (44:19, 21)

To Isaac too, for the sake of Abraham his father,
He assured the blessing of all mankind;
   he caused the covenant to rest on the head of
      Jacob. (44:22-23)

From him he produced a generous man
   who found favour in the eyes of all mankind,
beloved by God and men,
   Moses, of blessed memory. (45:1)

He made him the equal of the holy ones in glory
   and made him strong, to the terror of his enemies.

(45:2)

December 14

At the word of Moses he made the miracles stop,
  he raised him high in the respect of kings;
he gave him commandments for his people,
  and showed him something of his glory. (45:3)

December 15

He raised up Aaron, a holy man like Moses,
  his brother, of the tribe of Levi.
He made an everlasting covenant with him,
  and gave him the priesthood of the people. (45:6-7)

December 16

Mighty in war was Joshua son of Nun,
  successor to Moses in the prophetic office,
who well deserved his name,
  and was a great saviour of the Chosen People,
wreaking vengeance on the enemies who opposed
      him,
  and so bringing Israel into its inheritance. (46:1)

December 17

The judges too, each when he was called,
  all men whose hearts were never disloyal,
who never turned their backs on the Lord—
  may their memory be blessed! (46:11)

December 18

Samuel was the beloved of his Lord;
  prophet of the Lord, he instituted the kingdom,
  and anointed rulers over his people. (46:13)

David was chosen out of all the sons of Israel.
He played with lions as though with kids,
   and with bears as though with lambs of the flock.
While still a boy, did he not slay the giant,
   and relieve the people of their shame,
by putting out a hand to sling a stone
   which brought down the arrogance of Goliath?

(47:2-4)

For he called on the Lord Most High,
   who gave strength to his right arm
to put a mighty warrior to death,
   and lift up the horn of his people. (47:5)

In all his activities he gave thanks
   to the Holy One, the Most High, in words of glory;
he put all his heart into his songs
   out of love for his Maker. (47:8)

The Lord took away his sins,
   and exalted his horn for ever;
he gave him a royal covenant,
   and a glorious throne in Israel. (47:11)

Solomon reigned in a time of peace,
   and God gave him peace all round
so that he could raise a house to his name
   and prepare an everlasting sanctuary. (47:13)

The Lord would not go back on his mercy,
   or undo any of his words,
he would not obliterate the issue of his elect,
   nor destroy the stock of the man who loved him;
and so he granted a remnant to Jacob,
   and to David a root springing from him. (47:22)

And now bless the God of all things,
   the doer of great deeds everywhere,
who has exalted our days from the womb
   and acted towards us in his mercy. (50:22)

May he grant us cheerful hearts
   and bring peace in our time,
   in Israel for ages on ages. (50:23)

May his mercy be faithfully with us,
   may he redeem us in our time. (50:24)

December 28

Happy is he who busies himself with these things,
  and grows wise by taking them to heart. (50:28)

December 29

If he practices them he will be strong enough for
      anything,
  since the light of the Lord is his path. (50:29)

December 30

May your souls rejoice in the mercy of the Lord,
  may you never be ashamed of praising him. (51:29)

December 31

Do your work before the appointed time
  and he in his time will give you your reward. (51:30)

Daughters of St. Paul

MASSACHUSETTS
50 St. Paul's Ave., Jamaica Plain, Boston, MA 02130; **617-522-8911.**
172 Tremont Street, Boston, MA 02111; **617-426-5464; 617-426-4230.**

NEW YORK
78 Fort Place, Staten Island, NY 10301; **212-447-5071; 212-447-5086.**
59 East 43rd Street, New York, NY 10017; **212-986-7580.**
625 East 187th Street, Bronx, NY 10458; **212-584-0440.**
525 Main Street, Buffalo, NY 14203; **716-847-6044.**

NEW JERSEY
Hudson Mall—Route 440 and Communipaw Ave.,
Jersey City, NJ 07304; **201-433-7740.**

CONNECTICUT
202 Fairfield Ave., Bridgeport, CT 06604; **203-335-9913.**

OHIO
2105 Ontario Street (at Prospect Ave.), Cleveland, OH 44115;
216-621-9427.
616 Walnut Street, Cincinnati, OH 45202; **513-421-5733; 513-721-5059.**

PENNSYLVANIA
1719 Chestnut Street, Philadelphia, PA 19103; **215-568-2638;**
215-864-0991.

VIRGINIA
1025 King Street, Alexandria, VA 22314; **703-683-1741; 703-549-3806.**

SOUTH CAROLINA
243 King Street, Charleston, SC 29401.

FLORIDA
2700 Biscayne Blvd., Miami, FL 33137; **305-573-1618; 305-573-1624.**

LOUISIANA
4403 Veterans Memorial Blvd., Metairie, LA 70006; **504-887-7631;**
504-887-0113.
423 Main Street, Baton Rouge, LA 70802; **504-343-4057; 504-381-9485.**

MISSOURI
1001 Pine Street (at North 10th), St. Louis, MO 63101; **314-621-0346;**
314-231-1034.

ILLINOIS
172 North Michigan Ave., Chicago, IL 60601; **312-346-4228; 312-346-3240.**

TEXAS
114 Main Plaza, San Antonio, TX 78205; **512-224-8101; 512-224-0938.**

CALIFORNIA
1570 Fifth Ave., San Diego, CA 92101; **619-232-1442.**
46 Geary Street, San Francisco, CA 94108; **415-781-5180.**

WASHINGTON
2301 Second Ave., Seattle, WA 98121; **206-623-1320; 206-623-2234.**

HAWAII
1143 Bishop Street, Honolulu, HI 96813; **808-521-2731.**

ALASKA
750 West 5th Ave., Anchorage, AK 99501; **907-272-8183.**

CANADA
3022 Dufferin Street, Toronto 395, Ontario, Canada.